PARIS
The Capital

PARIS
The Capital

Text by Nicolas Chaudun
Translated by Max Berley
Photographs by François Bibal

Editions Pro Libris

PARIS
The Capital

There probably are 10,000 books on Paris in print and no doubt 10,000 more to come. One might wonder what a photo album could add to this avalanche. First, an eye, that of François Bibal. Bibal, who hangs from bridges and perches on the most unexpected summits, is perhaps the man most attached to the variations of the skies of Paris and to the special consistency of the "air de Paris." Second, the book offers an instant portrait of a city that is close to full realization. A city that has never ceased to rebuild within the limits of the fortifications drawn by Thiers 160 years ago.

Indeed, Paris changes from one book to the next, and, as Baudelaire complained, "faster, alas, than the heart of a mortal." The great transformation undertaken by Baron Haussman in the mid-nineteenth century, and later, the universal exhibitions, and later still, the ravings of seers like Le Corbusier, Sauvage or even Lurçat - who wanted to transform the Allée des Cygnes into an airfield - all this grinding has caused Parisians to mistake progress for a violation.

Already during the Enlightenment, the locals, mostly people from the provinces newly arrived in the capital, complained about everything. They complained about dust and mud, dirt and pestilence, and high prices, of course, but they also complained about the new architecture that was thought to be less flamboyant than that of the Sun King.

In his "Tableau de Paris," Louis-Sébastien Mercier jibed at the timid genius of the city's architects, criticizing all that we cherish today. The Sainte-Geneviève Basilica (The Panthéon), the Ecole de Chirurgie, the Odéon, none of these monuments found favor in his eyes. "They look, more or less, like temples. [...] One no longer dares to undertake a public monument ; the architect will come along with his columns and causes the kindly enterprise to recede."

This contradictory vigilance - a death sentence for the old combined with a fear of modernity - did not slow the efforts of the builders. At most it spared the landscape the warts of unnecessary urbanism. The pedestrian streets blocked by cement stubs are no more welcome here than are the roundabouts that are so common in the provinces.

The city's nobility, the majesty that tour guides describe from the decks of 1,000 panoramic tour buses, easily accommodates the successive onslaughts of myriad differences of style and of scale. The visitor travels along the arrogant cliffs of an endless avenue, when suddenly, to the left or right, a turret or the lopsided gable of an ancient house appears to surge out of thin air. The whole admiring world, it seems, strolls the Grand Boulevards, or is camped out on the esplanades, while this wonderful theater allows its cast - its true inhabitants - some very peaceful backstage areas in which to live. On the stage there is trepidation, but backstage, life goes on, beneath the meager foliage of impenetrable courtyards, between the imprecations of Portuguese concierges and the purring of cats sleeping on the warm hoods of cars. In this intimate disorder, which would appear to be deliberate but isn't, is born the "accidental beauty" of Paris, so eloquently sung by the poet Jean Cocteau.

But urban planners did have a role in creating this strange beauty, almost against their will. Swaying between repentance and flaunted visions, their debates can be read in the city's stones like a record of useless wars. It's a joyous sight. And the latest installments of the tale are not the least delightful. Without a doubt, the huge new neighborhood that is emerging from the wasteland of Tolbiac will be as much an homage to the royal squares as to the public housing of the suburban "Red Belt."

For our part, we will have to survive this paradox of grandeur and forgetfulness. One of the greatest qualities of this book is its mixture of permanence and promises for the future : The legendary stem of the Cité and the warning shots fired across the bows of La Défense and the Plaine Saint-Denis.

Paris is resplendent, but Parisians never cease to contest its changing splendor. And more than its splendors, its daily sweetness. Because, whatever else may be said of the city, it is a sweet place to live. Surely, there are blows exchanged on street corners, but these are fights without bloodshed. One also argues with rude meter maids, but only to be able to retell the struggle humorously to a newspaper vendor. At every turn, it seems, there is a café terrace at which to find refreshment or a square in which to unleash the children. On the margins of Paris's grand theater set, the city is a labyrinth of familiar landmarks. This is why the disappearance of a favorite bakery, or of one of the hardware stores known as "marchands de couleurs," is more acutely felt as a blow that the ravaging of a historic building that has been shabbily restored as a headquarters for a multinational company.

The press rather faithfully reflects this primacy of domestic concerns : There are fewer accounts of urban projects than of the merciless trench warfare between clothing stores and eating establishments. For our fathers, the local Breton charcuterie was the symbol of a whole art de vivre and it is with the same fervor that we worship our North African grocery store, without which we would be forced to fast on Sundays.

The Parisian will sign petitions to save a bookstore or a record shop that is threatened with extinction, but when it comes to cafés, he is ready to seize his rifle and his grenades. The Goncourt brothers led an insurrection against the destruction of the Café Riche and 100 years later, the novelist Antoine Blondin cursed the new owners of the Royal Saint-Germain.

Paris owes so much to its bistros. A collective lifting of the elbow among tobacco-filled mists takes on the cast of an ecumenical seminar, and the bust of the barmaid becomes the reincarnation of Saint Geneviève. The profanation of such a sanctuary cannot go unpunished.

Mitterrand's "great works" were acceptable because they were for show. The Parisian ends up grudgingly admiring the incomparable spectacle that is set before his eyes each day. How could he not ? He could almost break into song about its watered blondness, its capricious though rarely extreme climate, its distinguished gardens that are in bloom year-round. But he would also decry the armies of tourists in permanent ecstasy before such an embarrassment of riches. As for the rest, silence. The background, like the vestry of the café, is barred by a sign that says, "private, no admittance." One needs a refuge for trivial habits. When an outsider intrudes, the Parisian reverts to his grumpy ways. If a bulldozer were to destroy it, the Parisian would fall victim to nostalgia, a disease that is endemic to the banks of the Seine. To be less than 20 years-old and to hear oneself say to a friend : "In this place, where the dry cleaner now stands, there used to be a blue store where one can buy candies for one centime," is as delicious as it is humiliating. In fact, it's tacky.

I was six or seven when my father would wake me up in the middle of the night to go see hundreds of horses thundering along the cobblestones of Boulevard Lefebvre. Strong men in shirtsleeves were driving them to the abattoir. This cavalry was charging toward death at the slaughterhouse of Vaugirard. My father didn't mention that fact. As a result, my memory of these cavalcades is closer to the Roman races painted by Géricault than to the sad scenes of working life by Rosa Bonheur. I only saw this spectacle twice or three times, but that was enough to leave the impression of a ritual. Less than 10 years later the abattoir was closed. Barely had I entered high school than I had become a nostalgic witness, It seemed very early for me to claim membership of a generation that "had seen."

The Parisian likes to be seen. This vanity, compounded by a pathological fear, leads him to constantly seek new landmarks and invent new heroes. Yesterday, the stable boys shouted their orders on the Boulevards des Maréchaux, today the spider-like woodcutters can trim a plane tree in the blink of an eye with miniscule chainsaws.

But today, Gavroche is breaking windows in Mantes-la-Jolie, and the lords and ladies choose to spend New Year's Eve in London. The truth hurts: It has been 30 years since Parisians have made the headlines of history or those of the society pages. The Parisian's proverbial pride suffers from this, even if the prestige of the city still breeds envy.

Thus, the Parisian who lives inside the city's walls, the one who inhabits the area covered by the Métro's line 4, which connects the Porte de Clignancourt to the Porte d'Orléans without ever leaving city limits, can be distinguished from the suburbanite insofar as the Parisian doesn't feel the need to describe himself as such. The suburbanite claims to be a Parisian, even if he lives two hours from the Etoile. This is a place where a neighborhood is conceived as a village. Paris is a country ; one can be a Parisian from Belleville in the same way one can be a Frenchman from Normandy. Indeed, what does it matter where one was born ? The street vendor from Mali is just as Parisian as the high dignitary from the fifth arrondissement.

This fact has led some observers to decree that there were no more Parisians. Jean Favier has said that in today's cities, no one had a lineage of more than three generations. Without a doubt, sieges, famines and epidemics have long scrambled dynastic lines. The only ones who escape this rule are the grands bourgeois, who end up constituting a large part of a population that has been insidiously purged of its proletariat. These upper-class dynasties remain discrete, all the more since they often claim allegiance to the regions where they have their country houses, which take on the appearance of fiefdoms. Like their imitators - for the most part young executives seeking overseas jobs - they feel that they have pushed out the city their enemies, which include artists and idealists. In their wake, all of Paris assumes a siege mentality.

A finished city, a population under siege... if one were to believe the naysayers, Paris's heart now only beats to the tune of an end of reign paranoia. This would be taking little account of a hothouse that in the last 20 centuries has irradiated the entire world with its energy.

The time when a Parisian took food along for an excursion to Montrouge is long gone. Truth be told, the beur living in Sarcelles is every bit as poetic as the blouson noir of yesteryear. Revolutionary songs are sung in Arabic in the squats of the Plaine Saint-Denis, and Saint-Denis or Montrouge, Pantin or Issy ; it is all Paris. No one would think of contesting that the pastoral reunions of La Fontaine and Boileau in Auteuil belonged to the history of Paris. That being said, to pretend that Vincennes isn't Paris is to be short-sighted and to lack for memory. The dungeon of Charles V was nothing more than the vanishing point of a royal road of which the Bastille was the hinge, and the Louvre - as it is shown in the engravings of the Limbourg brothers - was its western point. And what about Sainte Geneviève, the city's patron saint. Was she not held up as the sweet "shepherdess of Nanterre" before she rebuffed Attila ? As for the Saint-Denis Basilica, it is a decidedly Parisian sanctuary. This isn't only because it contains the remains of France's kings - many of whom weren't exemplary citizens - but because it is here that, carrying his head in his hands, the saint who brought Christianity to Lutèce collapsed after having been tortured two leagues away, on the Mount of Mercury, which would thereafter be called the Mount of Martyrs, Montmartre.

It is in the suburbs that this city, the ancestral bramble bush of the Parisii, finds the youth and fury that it needs to thrive. Each night, the virtual gates of the périphérique are breached by a varied and fun-loving crowd. Their merry sounds travel down the avenues, encircle noble vestiges of the past, to finally echo into silence in dark alleys. With them, they carry the eternal romance of Paris. The soul of Paris, built century after century by these crowds, has little regard for the city's administrative boundaries.

The old village of Fontenay-sous-Bois, which gathers in the shadows of rickety warrens, could easily be mistaken for the old neighborhood of Vaugirard. What one finds there is the slang of the guardhouse, the language of the outer boundaries, and in the same way its inhabitants find consolation for the expensive prices that prevail at better addresses. And since the corner of the Rue des Morillons no longer echoes with the noise of mechanics, one must go to Vanves to shake motor oil-stained hands. Or perhaps to Levallois, which is haunted by the ghost of Boris Vian, would come here to fix his asthmatic cars. To continue to draw a distinction between the city and its suburbs is deny the evidence of the future. It is also to deny the past, which was built on successive encroachments.

One takes to dreaming that the old expansionism by decree will take over from the "overall scheme" now in practice and which creates a king of tarnished feudalism. One dreams that the Boulevard Périphérique, which squeezes the city's heart into the vestiges of its former fortifications, will be buried. And that a new Haussman will appear to give new life to the crown jewel.

The issue of enlarging the city crops up at regular intervals. The arguments against it are similar to those heard by Baron Haussman, when he planned to give the city a makeover. Nonetheless, the march of history will sweep these futile discussions away. Foremost among these concerns is the fear of creating a giant hog of a city that would be incapable of feeding its offspring. On the eve of World War I, Paris had a population of four million. Today, half that many remain. It would seem that the questions raised by the city's growth have already been answered. New frontiers will have to be drawn. This, however, will be child's play. These frontiers already exist. They are almost natural : To the west, the inferior bend of the Seine and Séguin, Saint-Germain, Puteaux and the Grande-Jatte Islands. To the south and east, the ribbon of fortified forward positions built by Thiers. This would only be a venial sin, a modest upheaval. The city has already more or less expanded to include the Bois de Boulogne and the Bois de Vincennes, the green lungs of Paris. The funny thing is that the shape of the city would not change. It would preserve its brain-shaped profile, which is fitting.

What good would it do ? Probably none, or rather, that would depend at the use made of the city. It would free the city from incarceration and to open it to its vassals. Paris is so beautiful, its nobility so contagious, that it would only take 20 years for it to domesticate the chaos that surrounds it. The city's arsenal of beauty stands ready. Better yet, it is already on the move in the Tolbiac neighborhood. A new city, extended toward the rising sun, is emerging from those banks. Its expansion has but one goal: To seal in stone the marriage of the Seine and the Marne. Just imagine Paris as a Rome with seven islands and a confluence of rivers as its gate.

I would like this album to be the last snapshot of an old melting pot that is ready to overflow. A survey before the inevitable transformation. After a gestation period, François Bibal would rub his poet's eyes and would seize his walking stick, but this time for a much longer trek. Dreaming is allowed, and Paris is the ideal place to do it. The stroll that you are invited to take in the following pages is proof of that. Indeed, it is impossible not to surrender to the golden hues of the incomparable skies of Paris, to the wise poetry of its facades and to the insolence of its esplanades...

All you need to do is to lift your eyes, and you can do so without fear because here dreams come while wide awake. Each day, you cross an avenue that strikes you as unremarkable. Then, one morning, the avenue is decorated with a hundred sculptures - displayed right there in the street and not in a museum. The statues will be packed away and replaced by the improvised orchestras of a street party and at the slightest provocation, fireworks will light up the sky.

Clearly, the city is prolix with her graces. She flirts. To shine is in her nature. And that no one can contest. She is never short of an argument whether it's smiling to unfortunate lovers or winking at drunken night owls. The scintillation of a carafe under the scattered foliage of a plane tree, the sight of a dome covered in gold sheet ; these lights could have earned her nickname. Paris is as much a "city of light" by the twinkle of its stones as by the random and wise cut of its street. Everything here radiates prosperity and savoir-faire. Everything - the domes and the steeples, the facades and colonnades, the zinc of the rooftops and that of the cafes, the quais, the peak of Montmartre seem to invite the world to witness the endless love affair between geography and man's genius. To love Paris is to love life. But life rarely keeps its promises. Paris always does. Noblesse oblige.

Nicolas Chaudun

Paris is a capital city. Squeezed into columns of cars along the Seine's banks, travelers brush by old and new stones, glass and steel. They raise their eyes to the Stade de France, the Opéra Bastille, the Grande Arche at La Défense, the Grand Louvre, the Grande Bibliothèque, the new buildings that Paris regularly erects to be deserving of its status as a capital. These are all huge and in harmony with the city's Grand Siècle style.

But part the red curtain and have a look backstage. Paris is a homeland, like homelands all over France and around the world. It has real inhabitants, some of whom were born here and who have real habits. It has schools and post offices, newspaper stands, and cafés with expressos and ham sandwiches. Parisians cross their city in the world's slowest buses. This gives them more time to admire the rooftops shining with rain. They gather at café terraces that are open until All Saints Day and they stroll in public gardens. This is their city and they love it. The city and its inhabitants offer each other the same freedom. This freedom has been torn away from Huns and Prussians and other invaders since the creation of Lutèce, 2000 years ago.

In song, Paris is a "blond," or the "queen of the world." In French movies it has been through many transformations. American movies, in a moving tribute, have shown apartments where through one window one could see the Eiffel Tower and through the other the Sacré Cœur. Are you for or against Buren's columns at the Palais-Royal ? Who cares. Armies of children have made it into a playground. Paris just shrugs, picks up its train and goes off to redecorate the hôtel Carnavalet.

Make a stop at the Pont-Neuf on a winter afternoon. In the distance, on the right bank embankment, cars whistle by like toys. A long and heavy barge carrying four pyramids of coal cuts through the green and greasy water. The sun sheds its rays on the golden stones of the Quai de la Mégisserie and on the terrifying towers of the Conciergerie. What you have before you is an incredible picture, one of which you might say, "Yes, but it's a photograph." Or, "Yes, but it's a painting." What you are really saying is that it looks like it is fake, an enhancement of reality. But this visual composition is real, quotidian, banal. Let yourself go: You are swimming in the universe. Because Paris is not just a capital, or a city, or a village, but a living being, emerging from the water. It has a huge heart, which beats in the entrails of earth and whose pounding resounds everywhere, in every square, in every street.

When I wanted to photograph her, she allowed me. And even if this wasn't always easy, as I always had to run after the sun or a cloud, my photographic journey through the city was a delight each day. Paris allowed herself to be seen and if you like these pictures, I will thank Paris for having given them to me.

François Bibal

Led by the architects Macary, Zublena, Regembal and Constantini, the Stade de France project doesn't end with the stadium itself. Taking advantage of a curb in the Saint-Denis Canal, an ambitious real estate program is expected to bring new life to this blighted neighborhood on the city's outskirts.

These days it's a cliché to compare the Stade de France to a kind of flying saucer. Nonetheless, nothing is more astounding than the landing of this beautiful alabaster ring in the middle of this industrial wasteland. With the help of France's 1998 World Cup victory, it only took six months for the stadium to become the symbol of French national harmony.

15

For a long time, the hill of Montmartre, which is named for the martyr Saint Denis and his companions, was but a landscape of underbrush dotted here and there with decrepit shacks. The domes of the Sacré Cœur may well make it the most well-known panorama of Paris, but Montmartre remains a village that jealously preserves its personality.

Page 17 (above). In 1929, the artist Francisque Poulbot transformed the garden of Bruant's house into a square. Four years later, vines were planted there, in memory of the "piccolo" that the winemaking nuns of the hill used to sell without compunction.

Page 17 (below). When the painter André Gill bought the Cabaret des Assassins, he placed on its front a sign decorated with a rabbit. When it was later taken over by Bruant, the former "Lapin à Gill" built its renown on customers such as Picasso and Modigliani.

Despite the shady commerce that made it famous, Pigalle remains a leading venue for music hall shows. The revues of the Moulin Rouge, immortalized by Toulouse-Lautrec, are an attraction known around the world.

Page 18. In 1873, the funds for the construction of the Sacré Cœur Basilica were voted by the National Assembly. Secular opposition and the fragility of its foundations delayed the end of the project until 1919. Even though it is relatively new, this strange monument has come to symbolize the 2,000 year-old city.

LA VILLETTE

La Villette : Only twenty years ago, this singsong name was neveruttered by resentful taxpayers without a sneer. For many, it was synonymous with "fiasco," "waste" or "boondoggle."

In the early 1960s, an assembly of unthinking bureaucrats decided to transform the picturesque slaughterhouse built by Baron Haussman in the mid-19th century into a gigantic killing assembly line, designed to refrigerate, eviscerate and butcher every bovine in France. But progress in refrigerated transportation and the development of regional slaughterhouses prevented the new complex at La Villette from becoming fully operational. The state monies spent on building the new slaughterhouse sank into a black hole. And, beginning in 1974, the secular reign of the cattle and horse traders ended there. The only traces that remain are a few bronze cow heads affixed to storefronts.

A complex of buildings resembling a space station then took over the neighborhood. La Cité des Sciences et de L'Industrie is its mothership and the Géode its main satellite. The architect, Bernard Tschumi, has also placed here and there scarlet follies, which could easily serve as the spaceship's intergalactic escort vessels.

The complex, which is devoted to the technologies of the future, opened its doors on the very day of the last passage near Earth of Haley's Comet, March 13, 1986. Despite the forbidding mass of the Cité de la Musique, which overwhelms the main entrance to the science complex, millions of children of all ages are drawn here each year to see the virtualization of the universe.

Indeed, from the confines of the largest hemispheric movie theater - the Géode - one can cruise the Milky Way or explore the Arctic ice flow. Nearby, the suspended carcass of the Agronaute, one of the early submarines, swarms with sailors in short trousers.

La Grande Halle des Boeufs and the old Bourse aux Cuirs host concerts, theater performances and art exhibits. Even the most jaded Parisian is forced to acknowledge the obvious : There is always something to do here.

Inaugurated in 1986, the Cité des Sciences et de l'Industrie receives 5 million visitors a year. This enormous building of glass and steel designed by Adrien Fainsilber is surrounded by moats and contains one of the largest aquariums in Europe.

La Villette was but an industrial wasteland when the project for a center devoted to the technologies of tomorrow was born. Connected to the Cité de la Musique, the Cité des Sciences et de l'Industrie has contributed more than any other project to the revitalization of eastern Paris.

Containing the largest hemispheric screen in the world, the Géode is a sphere of 36 meters in diameter, covered with 6,433 triangles of polished steel. The changing reflections of the park and the sky transform it into a permanent spectacle.

A rare survivor among the 60 pavilions built by Claude Nicolas Ledoux in 1783, the rotunda of La Villette has endured many vicissitudes before becoming the headquarters of the Commission du Vieux Paris. The restoration of the pool beneath it has restored its Palladian rigor.

A striking example of the devastating urbanism of the Gaullist era, the Cité des Flamands, Rue de Flandre, seems to crush its surroundings. In 1977, the very year it was finished, new zoning laws restricted buildings to more human scale.

With its alignment of plane trees, its creaking locks and its metal bridges, the Canal Saint-Martin is a perfect refuge for poets and the poor. Nonetheless, nothing remains of its past as a working-class neighborhood, other than the landmark and restored facade of the Hôtel du Nord.

LA BASTILLE

Only 25 years ago, one still spoke of the hoodlums of La Bastille as if evoking a horde of Genghis Khans on motorscooters. Specialty stores on Boulevard Richard-Lenoir, which paint motorcycle gas tanks and will chrome any cycle from exhaust pipe to handlebars, try to keep alive the days of the wild ride, but the Laverdas and Triumphs are silent now, and with them the revolutionary pulse of Paris.

For two hundred years the city's heart beat here, ever since July 14, 1789, when a crowd of subjects came to claim citizenship at the doors of the old prison and reduced it to rubble. It's a shame the old building is gone, though. One can only imagine what Viollet-le-Duc, the architect who restored Notre-Dame in the mid-19th century, might have done with the building.

In the years following the storming of the prison, many battles maintained the neighborhood's reputation for rebellion, particularly the bloody events of 1830 and 1848, whose victims are commemorated in bas-relief on the base of the Colonne de Juillet.

The monument witnessed even bloodier days during the Commune, in 1870-71. But the Génie de la Liberté, perched atop the column, "which takes flight while breaking its chains and spreading light," has progressively become the patron of the great labor-union marches of May 1. Red banners, not muskets, now snap beneath its wings, and more dancing than fighting unfolds today in its shadow.

The Faubourg Saint-Antoine, which remained a working-class neighborhood until the 1980s, still contains the workshops of furniture artisans. The area's courtyards and passages, littered with sawdust and metal shavings, its no-nonsense bistros, but especially its unrenovated lofts, had attracted many intellectuals and fashion creators. The nocturnal hubbub of Rue de Lappe and Rue Saint-Sabin seemed to be Paris's answer to Madrid's Movida.

The neighborhood's popularity attracted one of the symbolic gestures of which President François Mitterrand was so fond. In 1982, in the name of the democratization of culture, he announced the creation of a new opera house, which would replace the old Bastille train station. It was pitched as a "people's opera," which "would belong to the public, unlike the Opéra Garnier, a closed building that appears unbreachable." Paradoxically, the inauguration of this glass and steel iceberg - July 14, 1989, no less - announced the retreat from the area of its bohemian pioneers, who fled to Belleville or the outskirts of La République.

The Bastille neighborhood is now suffering the consequences of its new cultural status. It has become more bourgeois, but slowly. Its stealthy mutation, however, offers the delightful paradoxes of an interregnum, where the old and the new co-exist.

Page 29. The Génie de la Liberté, by Dumont, holds in one hand the broken chains of despotism, and in the other the torch of civilization. Despite its male touches, the turn of its hips earned the statue the decidedly female nickname of "Louloute" among the motorcycle gangs that used to gather at its feet.

Nothing more proud, or as intact, has survived the brilliant reign of Charles V. Even if Vincennes is not part of Paris, this is the Paris equivalent of the Tower of London.

The new library, the Bibliothèque de France, marks the beginning of the city's expansion eastward. The main point of its placement there was to replace a post-industrial desert with a beating heart, which would anticipate the unavoidable overflow of the city.

Page 37. It was the idea of this forest sanctuary, like an insular Eden, that determined François Mitterrand's choice of proposal for the new national library when the projects were presented. "Très grande", yet "très" archaic in its minimalist modernism, the library designed by Dominique Perrault set off a controversy that has not yet ended.

The strange seeded ramps of the Palais Omnisports de Bercy contain a huge modular room that can hold up to 17,000 people and allow 24 athletic events to take place at once. The Palais is also the venue for memorable concerts.

Page 39. Conceived by the architects Chemetov and Huidobro as the eastern door to Paris, the colossal portico of the Ministry of Finance plunges into the river. The double viaduct of Bercy, both a road and waterway, appears to surge from within.

The bell tower of the Gare de Lyon looks sad among the blocks of this new neighborhood dedicated to the service industry. However, the extra-flat roadway of the Pont Charles-de-Gaulle, of which it seems to form the axis, has restored something of the pre-eminence it once enjoyed in the area.

For centuries, in the wake of Louis XIVth's doctors, apothecary herbs have been grown here. The contrasts between the immaculate flower beds and the decrepit palmarium, and between the antique paleontology department and the futuristic Grande Galerie, make the Jardin des Plantes one of the most spellbinding places to stroll.

Page 43. The restoration of the old Galerie de l'Evolution by Chemetov and Huidobro gave an impulse to the effort to vulgarize the natural sciences. The most minute expressions of life on Earth are explained.

43

The Institut du Monde Arabe, which has been called a "vast and elegant lightbox", seems to hug the shores of the Seine. While its northern façade reflects the skyline of the Ile Saint-Louis, Jean Nouvel endowed its southern exposure with photoelectric screens that filter the sun.

The statue of Saint Geneviève on the Pont de la Tournelle, by Paul Landowski, is a reminder that in 885 the relics of the patron saint of Paris were displayed on the eastern tip of the Cité to protect Paris from Norman raids.

From the Square de L'Ile de France, which has become a memorial to those who perished in deportation, the prow of the Cité seems to carry the Ile Saint-Louis, the most noble sanctuary of France's Grand Siècle, in its wake like a ceremonial vessel.

Louis Le Vau built most of the hôtels of the Ile Saint-Louis. Around 1750, what is now the Quai de Béthune was still called "Quay des Balcons" because the architect had imposed this ornament then deemed sanitary on all the facades.

Pont Marie has nothing to do with the Virgin. It is named for the courageous entrepreneur, Christophe Marie, who obtained from Louis XIII the permission to unite, and build on, the two islets that form the basis of the Ile Saint-Louis, but with the provisio that he connect the island to shore by two symetrical bridges.

Quai d'Anjou. Breaking with the traditional configuration of Parisian homes, between courtyard and garden, the Hôtels of the Ile Saint-Louis, (Lauzun by Le Vau, right), turn toward the quais, allowing residents to the view and the fresh air carried by the river.

The changes undertaken by Baron Haussman can best be perceived from the sky. By substituting slate for zinc for tiles, the prefect made Paris into a rather calm gray-blue sea, from which the ships of history burst. (Notre-Dame, right ; Hôtel de Ville, left).

L'HÔTEL DE VILLE

You don't have to be a Parisian of old lineage to share with the locals a grudging sympathy for the Communards. One need only be propelled by a gust of inexplicable romanticism. An overwhelming despair must have driven the men and women of Ménilmontant and of Belleville in their quest for secession, and their rage must have been blinding for them to feel compelled to set alight some of the city's most noble monuments.

Among the many fires of the Semaine Sanglante of 1871, there is one that stands out as doubly absurd, that of the old city hall, the Hôtel de Ville. By reducing to ashes the beautiful Renaissance building, designed by the Italian architect Boccador, the Communards erased the immemorial symbol of the city's defiance.

It was here that in 1357, Etienne Marcel, another rebel, had installed the city's administration, with the intent of standing up to the monarchy's power. In addition, the Communards' fire destroyed all the city's birth records and with them the history of the capitals most humble residents.

After the fire, Paris attempted to recreate its memory by asking the architects Ballu and Deperthes to build a new city hall that would be a replica - though bigger - of the one lost to the flames. Their pastiche is almost a masterpiece, though the reception rooms are more accomplished than the façade. The front of the building is too white, too flat, perhaps, and has the effect of squashing the old Place de Grève, where generations of offenders to the king's law were tortured on the wheel.

Petrified in their alcoves, the statues of the city's most glorious sons stand guard, but no echo remains of those tortures, nor of the party in the square that greeted the birth of the king's son. On the other hand, the inside of the building transcends the academic style that prevailed at the time its creation, at the beginning of the Third Republic. It is a maze that meanders from hushed corridor to ornate reception room, the decoration of which is perfectly in keeping with the political mission to which it is assigned. The cinematic frescoes by Jean-Paul Laurens in the Salon Lobau, *La Répression de la Révolte des Maillotins, Etienne Marcel Protégeant le Dauphin or Louis XVI reçu par Bailly à l'Hôtel de Ville,* for example, remind out-of-towners that the people of Paris have made more than their share of history. Elsewhere in the building, there are parables and history lessons as interpreted by Bonnat, Puvis de Chavannes, Barrias or Carrier-Belleuse, none of which reach the artistic heights of Ingres or Delacroix, but who were undoubtedly the best official image-makers in France at the time.

But the pomp and ceremony fail to hide a more petty reality. Even as the city was celebrated in frescoes and crystal of Baccarat, Paris was paying dearly its insurrectional fever. Two tightly controlled prefects imposed their own law, in defiance of communal freedoms. This domination would end only in 1977, with the first election of a mayor of Paris.

By its size and its whiteness, the new Hôtel de Ville dominates the old Place de Grève, once the beating heart of the city. This extravagant "château" is still the secular symbol of the city - and its soul.

This is the emplacement of the "Maison aux Piliers," where in 1357 Etienne Marcel set up the city's bureau. The statue of the provost, by Jean Idrac, stands in the mayor's gardens, by the Seine. In the foreground, the Passerelle Saint-Louis, where year-round jugglers and buskers offer entertainment.

Begun in the waning days of the Gothic era, and finished in the waxing days of classicism, the Eglise Saint-Gervais-Saint-Protais, is a harmonious mélange of styles. Members of the Couperin family, whose house still stands Rue François-Miron, were organ-masters there from 1653 until the eve of the Revolution.

LE MARAIS

Le Marais takes pride in its reputation as the sanctuary of France's Grand Siècle, the 17th century. But when guidebooks describe the neighborhood as merely a living museum, they are only showing their short-sightedness and may be too lavish with their praise. Once declared unfit for habitation, the Marais has, like many other Paris neighborhoods, been the victim of a cleaning operation that took little account of its ghosts. And even if the remains of its 1,000-year history draws museumgoers, the neighborhood has maintained a lively population.

Beginning in the twelfth century, the area was used for cultivation, following the arrival of the Knights Templar, who built their headquarters on the outskirts of what was then a swamp. King Charles V was responsible for the area's development. He installed here the menagerie and famous gardens of the Hôtel Saint-Pol. The troops garrisoned at the Bastille kept a watchful eye, even as they controlled the road to the castle of Vincennes, where the king sought refuge when the populace became too restive.

In the king's wake came many court dignitaries, including the Conétable de Clisson, in the fourteenth century, a companion of the famed knight Dugesclin, whose sumptuous Hôtel remains rue des Archives. From then on, the Marais remained in fashion until the death of the Sun King, Louis XIV, in 1715. As a result, all of the kingdom's greatest architects were drawn to the Marais to claim their share of posterity. Lescot, Bruant, Mansart, Lepautre, Boffrand, Delamair and many others defined for centuries to come the archetype of the Parisian house, less a palace than a city château, trapped between a courtyard and a garden, and which only yields its closed gate to the curiosity of passers-by.

The lords of yesteryear were happy to live alongside artisans, shops and taverns, where their valets came to curse their masters. And the help needed somewhere to live. That is why tiny houses are gathered together, bringing some visual relief to the majestic layouts of the palaces. As a result, when the nobility moved to the west of the city, in the eighteenth century, the little people took over the townhouses from their masters. But many painted ceilings and gilded walls suffered from this transfer of ownership as the industrious lower classes subdivided the rooms and ostentatious salons of the upper classes. Nonetheless, the contrast between the utilitarianism of the working classes and the grandeur of the leisure class was what until recently lent Le Marais much of its charm.

But by changing status, many of the Hôtels of the aristocracy - there remain about 100 - were able to survive. For the most part, the Marais has managed to prevent the rising ranks of the government administration, which is always on the lookout for imposing buildings, from flooding the neighborhood. And, in light of the unfortunate restoration work the government has done on some of its most recent conquests - L'Hôtel d'Albret, which now houses the City of Paris's cultural affairs office - this is undoubtedly a felicitous development. Only the Rabbis and the Kosher grocers of Rue des Rosiers, who have held on heroically for more than a century, can claim the status of native.

Page 57. There are few like it. One stands Rue Volta and two Rue François-Miron, no more. But this ancient dwelling on the corner of Rue des Barres and Rue du Grenier-sur-l'Eau almost disappeared in the 1970s.

The former Hôtel of the archbishops of Sens suffered greatly from a botched restoration. Nonetheless, it remains a prime example of Parisian civil architecture of the end of the Middle Ages.

Page 58 (above). An exemplar of the Counter-Reformation style propagated by the Jesuits, Eglise Saint-Paul-Saint-Louis's Dome stands 55 meters high. Its windows allow abundant light to enter. When Madame de Sévigné came to listen to the sermons of Bourdaloue, she said she was "transported" and "charmed" by the building's brightness.

Page 58 (below). Built between 1625 and 1630, the former dwelling of Sully, a faithful minister of Henri IV, is now home to the Caisse Nationale des Monuments Historiques et des Sites.

The prototype of the royal square, Place des Vosges is the paragon of architecture under Louis XIII, particularly by its combination of brick and stone.

A discrete Renaissance house, the Hôtel de Donon was built for one of the king's administrators and his wife, the daughter of the famous ceramics maker Girolamo Della Robbia. Today it contains the Cognacq-Jay collection, devoted to the decorative arts of the eighteenth century.

Page 63 (above). Hôtel de Vigny was designated a national treasure after painted beams and a ceiling by Nicolas Loir were discovered. Like its neighbor, Hôtel Duret de Chevry, its was built for an unscrupulous financier, whose ostentation and arrogance was to prefigure the splendor of Fouquet.

Page 63 (below). The Hôtel Carnavalet, by Pierre Lescot et Jean Goujon and many times rearranged, was Madame de Sévigné's favorite abode. Later, Baron Haussmann acquired it on behalf of the city and installed the Musée Historique de Paris.

Hôtel de Soubise is a pure masterpiece, the apotheosis of an architect, Pierre-Alexis Delamair, who harmonized its entrance facade with the extraordinary colonnade in the courtyard, creating a theatrical effect that has no parallel among Parisian homes. In 1808, Napoleon placed the national archives here.